HISTORY OF FUN STUFF

The 4-1-1 on Phones!

by Kama Einhorn
illustrated by Mark Borgions

Ready-to-Read

Simon Spotlight
New York   London   Toronto   Sydney   New Delhi

SIMON SPOTLIGHT

An imprint of Simon & Schuster Children's Publishing Division
1230 Avenue of the Americas, New York, New York 10020
This Simon Spotlight edition October 2015
For information about special discounts for bulk purchases, please contact Simon & Schuster Special Sales at
1-866-506-1949 or business@simonandschuster.com.
Manufactured in the United States of America 0915 LAK
2 4 6 8 10 9 7 5 3 1
Library of Congress Cataloging-in-Publication Data
Einhorn, Kama, 1969-
The 4-1-1 on Phones! / by Kama Einhorn ; illustrated by Mark Borgions.
pages cm. — (History of fun stuff)
Audience: Grades K–3.
1. Telephone—Juvenile literature. I. Borgions, Mark, illustrator. II. Title.
TK6165.E55 2015
621.386—dc23
2015000888
ISBN 978-1-4814-4405-7 (hc)
ISBN 978-1-4814-4404-0 (pbk)
ISBN 978-1-4814-4406-4 (eBook)

CONTENTS

CHAPTER 1
The First Phones

Brr-ing! Brr-ing! Answer the phone—it's for you! If you take this call—that is, if you read this book—you'll learn the amazing history of the telephone. Here's one fast fact for you: The word "telephone" is made of the Greek words for "far" *(tele)* and "sound" *(phone)*. That makes sense, doesn't it? Think of all the ways that the telephone makes your life easier. Without telephones, it would be hard to let your parents know that your sports practice is running late. Without telephones, how could you call your grandmother to say happy birthday? Telephones are a really big part of our lives . . . but how did they come to be?

It has always been important for people to be able to communicate over long distances. For centuries this was done with smoke signals or the sound of drums, letters carried from one place to another, or messengers sent to deliver news. These methods were all used before electricity was more common in the nineteenth century.

There is, however, a phone that can be made without electricity. You might have even made one before. All you need are two tin cans or paper cups and a piece of string. Simply connect the string to the inside bottom of each can or cup, pull it tight, and then speak into one end. Someone on the other end will be able to hear what you said. Unfortunately, this phone only works over short distances.

Most historians consider Alexander Graham Bell the official inventor of the telephone. But other scientists before him helped make the invention possible. For instance, before Bell invented the telephone, Samuel Morse developed the electric telegraph in the 1830s.

The electric telegraph was a little like a long-distance typewriter. It used Morse code, which was a code of long and short pulses ("dots" and "dashes") made by electric current. Each combination of pulses stood for a different letter.

Then along came Alexander Graham Bell. Bell was born in 1847 in Scotland, though his family later moved to Canada. By 1871, he was living in Boston, Massachusetts. From a young age, Bell was interested in speech. His mother was almost deaf, and his father was a speech teacher. Bell became an expert on acoustics—the study of sound. As a young man, he took what he knew about the electric telegraph and added the element of sound.

Bell's harmonic telegraph, or musical telegraph, let telegraph companies send several messages at once. But Bell had another idea. He wanted to invent a device that used electricity to transmit speech.

Remember the tin-cup-and-string phone? Bell's invention uses the same basic idea—sound travels through a line. But Bell added electricity, which was, at the time, a pretty new field itself. It's hard to imagine today because electricity is such a major part of our lives, but back in the

1870s, even electric light bulbs were rare. It would take until 1925 before half of the homes in the United States had electricity.

Bell didn't really know that much about electricity, so he hired an electrician, Thomas Watson, to help him with his new invention.

But at the same time that Bell and Watson were working away to invent the telephone, an American inventor named Elisha Gray was working on . . . the telephone. And both Bell and Gray wanted the patent for their invention. *What's a patent?* you may be wondering.

A patent is issued by the government and protects an idea, giving inventors

ownership over their ideas so no one can steal them or take credit for them. Bell filed his patent application first, just hours before Gray filed a caveat, or intent to file a patent, on February 14, 1876. So Bell was the one to get the patent for it. For that reason, he is known as the inventor of the telephone.

On March 10, 1876, just a few weeks after he filed his patent application, Bell spoke the first words to ever be heard over a telephone to his partner Watson. Bell's words were "Mr. Watson, come here. I want to see you." Watson was able to hear Bell through the early telephone even though he was in a different room.

If you had been the person to make that first phone call, what would you have said?

Soon the Bell Telephone Company was formed, and the first permanent phone wires were installed. Can you imagine how exciting that must have been?

Businesspeople quickly realized how much potential this invention carried— they knew that once the word got out about telephones and the technology became more advanced, it wouldn't be long before the telephone business became a big money-maker. Right away, different companies began fighting over the technology and patents, just as phone companies continue to compete for customers today.

But Bell wasn't interested in that part of things. He just wanted to keep doing what he loved, which was studying science and inventing new technologies. So he left the Bell Company and moved on. He wound up being granted twenty-nine more patents for his various inventions!

tetrahedral kite

hydrofoil

vacuum jacket respirator

CHAPTER 2
Ring-a-ling

Today many people go online if they are looking for a phone number, but as you can imagine, that wasn't always the case! For more than a hundred years, before the Internet, people used telephone books to find numbers. The first telephone book was published in 1878. It was one page long and had only fifty names! Phones were mostly found in offices or businesses. But that, too, was about to change. It turns out those businesspeople were right when they predicted that the telephone business was going to be booming. And by 1918 there were more than ten million phones in service in the United States and many of these phones were in people's homes.

As the popularity of phones grew, they weren't just used in homes or businesses. Phones were even appearing outside! The first pay phone was set up in public in 1889. You don't see too many pay phones around today, but there are still some out there. You put a coin in the slot, and then hear a dial tone and make your call.

Have you ever used a pay phone?

As more people got phones and the invention continued to change the world, the look of phones changed too. In the 1890s there was the "candlestick phone." It was separated into two pieces—a mouthpiece and a receiver. Later the design changed so that you could listen and talk out of the same piece. By 1919 to make a call, you could also use a rotary phone. It wasn't until 1963 that people began using push-button phones. Today almost all phones are push button or touch screen. But one important thing hasn't changed at all: Since the 1960s, Americans have used phones to call 9-1-1 in an emergency.

early candlestick phone

later candlestick phone

rotary phone

push-button phone

cordless phone

cell phone

CHAPTER 3
Phones on the Move

By the 1940s many people had phones in their homes or offices, and you could often find a pay phone outside. But people couldn't use phones while they were on the move. All that changed with the car phone. The car phone, which used radio signals, was invented in 1946. The first one weighed eighty pounds, and a big part of its machinery had to be stored in the car's trunk!

Many people thought things couldn't get any cooler than the car phone. But then in 1973, Martin Cooper, a Motorola company engineer—inspired partly by Captain Kirk and his "communicator" on the TV show *Star Trek*—invented the first cell phone. The way people used phones was about to change forever.

Cooper knew people wanted to use phones anywhere, anytime, not just in their cars. Cooper used the cell phone he'd invented to make the first-ever cell-phone call in public. On a New York City sidewalk in front of a crowd of reporters, he spoke into a cell phone the size of a giant shoe.

And who did he call? His main competitor, of course—Joel Engel at Bell Labs. He said, "Joel, this is Marty. I'm calling you from a cell phone, a real handheld portable cell phone."

When they finally went on sale to the public in the early 1980s, Motorola DynaTAC phones cost around $4,000— about $9,000–$10,000 in today's money. And they took ten hours to charge—for around thirty minutes of conversation!

CHAPTER 4
Phones Get Smart

So a new chapter of telephone history had begun. The cell phone had been invented in 1973. But it took more than ten years for cell phones to be sold to the public. Why? The phone companies had to work with the government to set up the network, or system, needed for cell phones to work on a large scale. It was a complicated process that took a long time to figure out. It wasn't until that was settled in 1983 that people were able to start buying and using cell phones.

But it wasnt just mobile phones—other advances in telephone technology were on their way.

In the 1960s answering machines hit the shelves. By 1983 the first digital answering machine had appeared.

Answering machines are not as common today because voicemail is now built into our phones, but for many years answering machines were a staple in homes and businesses. And what about caller ID? These days, nearly every phone has it, but it wasn't until the mid-1990s that it became popular.

As all of these advances were happening, the popularity of cell phones was also soaring. New types of cell phones came on the market during the late 1990s, with features like long battery life. By 1997, if you owned a Nokia cell phone, you could even play a game called Snake on your phone. As time went on, more and more cell phones got smarter and smarter, being able to send and receive e-mails and even browse the web.

Then in 2007, Steve Jobs, the cofounder of Apple, presented the iPhone. It combined a mobile phone, a camera, Internet capabilities, a music player, and a touch screen so you could go online on your personal handheld wireless computer. Soon smartphones were everywhere, and on all of these new devices you could play games, send text messages, take pictures, and, of course, talk.

Speaking of being smart, cell phones today have their own central computer with technology more powerful than what was used during the moon landing in 1969! Think about it: Each of these phones has more processing power than a rocket ship that flew to the moon and back.

And it seems like people are always lining up for the next generation—the new batch—of cell phones. Almost every year companies unveil their new inventions with great suspense and fanfare.

Cell-phone fans hold their breath as they wait to find out what it will be. Cameras flash and reporters ask questions. People can't wait to have the latest and greatest devices and technology available. With all the new technology out there, phones are smarter than ever. Maybe they should be called genius phones.

You may have had a giggle while reading this book, thinking about some of the phones from the past. But what will kids in the future say when they learn about the phones we use today? What new kinds of communication tools do you think *they* might be using? Scientists are already developing the technologies for some amazing things. What are some of the things you'd like to see the phone of the future do?

Congratulations! You've come to the end of this book. You are now an official History of Fun Stuff Expert on phones. Go ahead and impress your friends and family with your off-the-hook knowledge about where these nifty little talking machines came from. And next time the phone rings, think about all the people that invented the technologies that keep your friends and family close—as near as your ear!

Hey, kids! Now that you're an expert on the history of phones, turn the page to learn even more about phones and some anatomy, social studies, and math along the way!

Have You Heard? The Incredible Science of Hearing

You might not think about it all the time, but your ears work really hard so that you can hear that "hello" on the other end of the phone! But how exactly do we hear?

Your ears are divided into three main parts: the **outer**, **middle**, and **inner ear**. Each part has an important role in helping sound reach your brain!

The outer ear is closest to the outside of your body and is made up of several parts. The **auricle,** or **pinna,** is probably what you mean when you talk about the ear; it's the part that you can see on the outside of your head. The auricle is specially designed to capture sound so it can travel to the next part of your ear: the ear canal. The **ear canal** is like a tiny tunnel that helps funnel sound inward to the eardrum. Just like how a real drum vibrates when you hit it with a drumstick, the **eardrum** translates sounds into vibrations.

hammer
anvil
stirrup
cochlea
auditory nerve
auricle
eardrum
ear canal

Next the vibrations from the eardrum travel to the middle ear, which has three bones in it—the tiniest bones in your body! The **hammer**, **anvil**, and **stirrup** bones make those vibrations even bigger, kind of like turning up the volume on a cell phone.

These vibrations then travel to the inner ear. Unlike the first two parts of the ear, the inner ear is full of fluid. Here there is a special organ called the **cochlea**, which is shaped like a snail! Inside, the cochlea has tiny hairs, or **cilia**, that move when sound vibrations hit them. The cilia generate nerve impulses—special electrical signals that travel from the **auditory nerve** to the brain, where your brain interprets the signals as sound.

Ahoy! Telephone Greetings from Around the World

In America today we normally say hello or hi when answering the phone, but in other countries people have many different ways of answering a call!

- In Brazil most people say *alô* (ah-LO), which means "hello," to answer the phone. It is common for people in Brazil to say "uh" while the person on the other end is talking. They do this to show that they're still on the line.
- In South Korea you would answer the

phone with *yeoboseyo* (yoh-BOH-say-yoh) or "hello" in English. South Korea is home to Samsung, one of the largest mobile phone and electronics companies in the world, which was founded in 1938.

- In Japan they say *moshi moshi* (MOH-shee, MOH-shee) when answering the phone. It's considered very rude to answer or talk on the phone while walking in Japan. In fact, the "silent mode" function on mobile phones is called "manner mode" in Japan.

• In Spain people answer with *dígame* (DEE-gah-may), which means "speak to me." Unlike in Japan, people in Spain commonly answer the phone during meetings and while eating in restaurants!

• In Sweden most people answer the phone by stating their name. Telephones came early to Sweden in 1877, and the country really embraced the new technology. Today, adults can even file their income tax returns via text message!

• In Turkey you would answer the phone with *buyurun* (BOO-yoo-roon) or "I'm listening to your call." But *buyurun* doesn't just have one meaning! In Turkish this word can mean "May I help you?" when you enter a shop, "Come in" when answering the door, or even "Have a seat" when a friend is visiting.

45

The Pie Chart: A Slice of Facts

Pie charts can be a helpful tool for organizing facts in an easy-to-understand way. Cell-phone companies use pie charts to make important business decisions, like what kind of apps to make next. But making a pie chart isn't hard—you might say it's easy as pie!

First we start with our data. **Data** is a collection of information or facts that researchers gather. For example, we asked ten people, "What kind of app do you use most often on your smartphone: games, e-mail, or music?" Each person chose one kind of app, and their responses (our data) were tallied in the table below.

Games	E-mails	Music	Total
2	3	5	10

In a pie chart, we split a circle into **sectors**, or little pie slices that represent our data. Since there were three possible answers to the question we asked, there will be three sectors in our pie chart!

Next we convert our data into **fractions**, or parts of the whole. In a fraction, the **denominator**, or bottom number, stands for the total parts; here our denominator is ten, since we asked ten people about their favorite kind of app. The **numerator**, or top number, stands for the different parts; here the numerators would be two for games, three for e-mail, and five for music.

Now we can make the following fractions: 2/10 of people used games the most, 3/10 of people used e-mail the most, and 5/10 of people used music the most.

To figure out how big each sector of our pie chart should be, we look at our denominator (ten) and divide a circle into that many equal parts.

Then we use different colors to shade in our fractions. We'll color two slices blue for games, three slices green for e-mail, and five slices red for music.

Now that the chart is colored in, we can add a title: "Most Often Used Kinds of Apps in 2015." The **title** is very important—it says what our chart is about! Next we add a **key**, which explains what each colored sector of the pie chart represents.

And there you have it! Ready for your next business meeting?

most often used kinds of apps in 2015

- Games
- e-mail
- music

Being an expert on something means you can get an awesome score on a quiz on that subject! Take this

HISTORY OF PHONES QUIZ

to see how much you've learned.

1. You can make a homemade phone using cups or tin cans and what?

    a. string   b. badgers   c. eggplants

2. What device did Samuel Morse invent in the 1830s?

    a. telephone   b. electric telegraph   c. iPhone

3. What was the name of Alexander Graham Bell's assistant?

    a. Thomas Watson   b. William Tell   c. John Adams

4. A paper from the government that says an inventor owns a specific idea is called a what?

    a. applesauce   b. modifier   c. patent

5. By 1918, how many telephones were in service in the United States?

    a. more than 27   b. more than 10 million   c. more than 3 billion

6. When was the pay phone invented?

    a. 2002   b. 1910   c. 1889

7. The car phone, invented in 1946, used what kind of signals to operate?

    a. radio signals   b. sound waves   c. telepathic signals

8. Push-button phones weren't invented until what year?

    a. 1992   b. 1889   c. 1963

9. Who invented the first cell phone?

    a. Susan B. Anthony   b. Martin Cooper   c. Joel Engel

10. A cell phone that allows you to play games, send text messages, and take pictures, and that has other computer-like functions is known as a what?

    a. smartphone   b. candlestick   c. rocket phone

Answers: 1. a   2. b   3. a   4. c   5. b   6. c   7. a   8. c   9. b   10. a